Get Money Meta

Mastering the Meta Marketplace

Get Money Meta

Mastering the Meta Marketplace

Errol Hassell

Published in USA by Trinity Publishing Company
Paperback ISBN: 978-1-964707-57-0

Book Cover by Trinity Publishing Company
Editing and Formatting by Trinity Publishing Company

Disclaimer:

The "Get Money Meta: Mastering the Meta Marketplace" group is intended as an educational resource for individuals and organizations seeking to enhance their team-building skills and improve team performance. This group provides practical advice, real-life examples, and strategies for personal and team growth; however, results may vary based on individual and team dynamics, commitment, and application of the strategies discussed.

The information shared within this group, including posts, comments, and discussions, reflects the personal experiences and opinions of contributors and should not be construed as professional or legal advice. Members are encouraged to seek additional resources and professional guidance specific to their unique situations.

By joining and participating in the group, members acknowledge that the administrators, moderators, and contributors are not liable for any direct or indirect results of implementing the strategies shared here. Success and outcomes depend on individual and team efforts, and members assume full responsibility for any decisions or actions taken based on information provided within the group.

Dedication

I want to give special thanks to Andi Scott, who has walked this journey with me. Her unwavering support and encouragement have been invaluable, and I am grateful for her wisdom throughout this process. Her expertise and guidance have been instrumental in helping me navigate the challenges along the way.

ACKNOWLEDGMENT

To every moderator and administrator on the Get Money Meta Team let's continue to grow. Your hard work and dedication have truly made a difference in our community. Together, we can achieve even greater success in the future. I appreciate the what each of you provide on a daily basis to make our team successful. Thank you for your commitment and passion towards our goals.

INTRODUCTION

Once upon a time, in New York City, there lived an ambitious man named Errol, also known as Wave Moneyy. He was known for his funny and motivating social media posts. Wave Moneyy has a knack for finding unique opportunities to make money. One day, while scrolling through Facebook, he stumbled upon a group called "Money Makers." He was intrigued by the name and decided to join the group to see what it was all about. To his surprise, he discovered that the group was a community of like-minded individuals who shared tips, strategies, and success stories about making money online. As he took a deeper look into the group's discussions, he realized that many members were using social media as a platform to generate income. They were leveraging the power of social media to build businesses, sell products, and offer services. They started charging people to make engagement posts, so Wave Moneyy stopped participating but took the group's example as inspiration and decided to pursue this opportunity further by starting his own group.

He began by showing off his skills as a graphic designer to create custom logos and social media graphics for his new group. He showcased his work by creating the group's logo and making it the profile picture. Wave Moneyy received positive feedback and inquiries from interested clients, and many people joined his new Facebook group. He began putting together a team of administrators and moderators. With each successful project, his reputation within the group was visibly growing, and more people were reaching out for his services. He soon realized that there was a demand for social media management, so he expanded his offerings to include managing Facebook pages and running advertising campaigns for businesses.

Wave Moneyy got the idea to unite with his administrator, Andi Scott, to create content that he uses on Facebook and YouTube to monetize the two of them. Their dedication and hard work paid off, and they began earning a substantial income through their Facebook ventures, and the two began mentoring and guiding other members of the group who wanted to follow a similar path. As the Get Money Meta group flourished, Wave Moneyy became an integral part of its community. He shared his experiences and insights and even collaborated with other members on joint ventures.

As Andi Scott, the administrator, did interviews, Wave Moneyy did the editing and placed them on YouTube. He also used the content for Facebook using the Club House app. The Get Money Meta group became different from other groups because of the work the two were putting in. It also became a hub of knowledge and support, where people from all walks of life came together to learn, grow, and make money on Facebook. The group wasn't just about making money for Wave Moneyy and Andi Scott. They soon discovered that the true value of the group lay in the connections they both made and the knowledge they gained. The friendships they formed with fellow entrepreneurs became an invaluable source of inspiration and motivation. Over time, their success story became an inspiration for others in the group. Members started realizing that with the right mindset, determination, and a supportive community, they too could achieve their financial goals through Facebook. As time went by, the Get Money Meta group continued to thrive, attracting more members, providing endless opportunities for individuals to monetize their skills and passions, and interviewing members about their lives, businesses, and whatever they wanted the world to hear.

Wave Moneyy's journey from a curious member to a successful entrepreneur became a legend within the group, inspiring generations of ambitious dreamers to turn their Facebook profiles into profitable ventures. And so, the story of Wave Moneyy and the Get Money Meta group serves as a reminder that with the right mindset, a supportive community, and the power of social media, anyone can unlock their potential and create a pathway to financial success. The group continues to grow, with new members joining every day and sharing their success stories and advice with one another. Wave Moneyy's legacy lives on as a beacon of hope for those looking to break free from traditional career paths and pursue their passions on their own terms. Until you make it, keep moving forward on the 9–5 that you are blessed to have, but always keep your eyes on the ultimate goal of financial freedom and independence. The Get Money Meta group is there to support and motivate you every step of the way.

TABLE OF CONTENTS

01 META PLATFORMS

In chapter one, we will dive into the rise of Meta platforms and their impact on the digital economy. We explore the concept of the metaverse and its significance, as well as provide an overview of the different Meta platforms and the earning potential they offer. By understanding the foundations of Meta and its ecosystem, readers will be well-equipped to navigate the subsequent chapters and embark on their journey to financial success in the Meta marketplace.

Understanding the rise of Meta and its impact on the digital economy. In recent years, Meta has emerged as a dominant force in the digital landscape, revolutionizing the way we connect, communicate, and consume content. Formerly known as Facebook, Meta has transformed into a metaverse company, aiming to build a virtual reality-based social and economic ecosystem. This chapter provides an introduction to Meta platforms, exploring their rise and examining the profound impact they have on the digital economy.

THE EMERGENCE OF META

Meta's transformation from Facebook into a metaverse company represents a significant shift in the tech industry. Mark Zuckerberg's vision for a connected and immersive online world has led to the creation of Meta platforms that transcend traditional social media networks. By embracing virtual reality, augmented reality, and other immersive technologies, Meta aims to redefine how we interact with digital content and each other.

THE METAVERSE CONCEPT

The concept of the metaverse refers to a collective virtual shared space where users can interact with a computer-generated environment and other users in real-time. Meta's ambition is to create a metaverse that offers seamless integration of virtual and physical realities, blurring the boundaries between the digital and physical worlds. This vision opens up exciting possibilities for entertainment, communication, commerce, and more. As technology continues to advance, Meta's metaverse has the potential to revolutionize how people interact with each other and their surroundings.

IMPACT ON THE DIGITAL ECONOMY

The rise of Meta platforms has had a profound impact on the digital economy, creating new opportunities for individuals and businesses alike. With billions of users and an extensive ecosystem, Meta platforms have become a lucrative marketplace for content creators, entrepreneurs, advertisers, and developers. The increasing popularity of virtual reality and augmented reality experiences opens up new avenues for monetization and innovation.

Exploring the different Meta platforms and their earning potential.

META PLATFORMS OVERVIEW

Meta encompasses a range of platforms, each serving different purposes within the metaverse. This section provides an overview of the key Meta platforms, including Meta Social, Meta Horizon, and Meta Workrooms, highlighting their unique features and functionalities.

META SOCIAL

Meta Social, formerly known as Facebook, remains one of the most prominent Meta platforms. It offers a wide range of social networking features, including profiles, news feeds, groups, and messaging. Content creators on Meta Social can leverage their presence to engage with audiences, build communities, and monetize their content through various means.

META HORIZON

Meta Horizon is a virtual reality-based platform that allows users to explore immersive environments, interact with other users, and participate in virtual experiences. For content creators, Horizon offers opportunities to design and develop their own virtual spaces, create games, and monetize their creations.

META WORKROOMS

Meta Workrooms is a collaboration platform designed for remote work and virtual meetings. It provides virtual meeting spaces where users can connect, collaborate, and share content in a virtual environment. This platform opens up possibilities for remote workers, entrepreneurs, and businesses to connect and work together in an immersive setting.

EARNING POTENTIAL ON META PLATFORMS

Meta platforms offer various avenues for earning money. Content creators can monetize their presence through advertising, brand partnerships, sponsorships, and virtual goods sales. Developers can create and sell virtual assets, games, and experiences. Entrepreneurs can build businesses within the metaverse, offering products and services to the growing user base. The earning potential on Meta platforms is vast, and this chapter explores the different strategies and opportunities available.

02 SETTING THE FOUNDATION FOR SUCCESS

In chapter two, we explore the process of setting the foundation for success on Meta platforms. By assessing your skills and interests, researching Meta platforms, evaluating market demand, setting financial goals, and developing a strategic plan, you will be well-prepared to embark on your journey towards earning money on Meta. The chapter emphasizes the importance of aligning your abilities with the right platform and provides guidance on identifying monetization opportunities. With a strong foundation in place, you will be ready to take the next steps towards financial success in the Meta metaverse.

Assessing your skills and interests to identify the right Meta platform for you.

UNDERSTANDING YOUR SKILLS AND INTERESTS

Before diving into the world of Meta platforms, it is essential to assess your skills and interests. Each Meta platform offers unique opportunities, and aligning your abilities with the right platform will increase your chances of success. Consider your expertise in areas such as content creation, virtual reality development, entrepreneurship, or remote collaboration. Identifying your strengths will help you choose the Meta platform that best suits your talents.

RESEARCHING META PLATFORMS

Conduct thorough research on the different Meta platforms available. Explore Meta Social, Meta Horizon, Meta Workrooms, and other emerging platforms to understand their features, user base, and monetization options. Consider the type of content or services you wish to offer and assess which platform aligns best with your goals. Take note of successful creators and entrepreneurs who have found their niche within each platform to gain insight into the possibilities.

EVALUATING MARKET DEMAND

Assess the market demand for the type of content or services you plan to offer on Meta platforms. Investigate the audience size, engagement levels, and competition within your chosen niche. Understanding the market demand will allow you to tailor your offerings and strategies to meet the needs and preferences of the Meta platform users.

Setting financial goals and developing a strategic plan for earning money on Meta.

SETTING FINANCIAL GOALS

Establish clear financial goals for your journey on Meta platforms. Determine how much money you aim to earn and the timeline for achieving your goals. Consider both short-term and long-term objectives. Setting specific, measurable, achievable, relevant, and time-bound (SMART) goals will provide you with a clear direction and motivation to succeed.

RESEARCHING MONETIZATION STRATEGIES

Explore the various monetization strategies available on Meta platforms. These can include advertising revenue, brand partnerships, sponsorships, virtual goods sales, subscription models, and more. Research successful creators and entrepreneurs who have effectively monetized their presence on Meta platforms and learn from their strategies. Determine which monetization methods align with your content or services and incorporate them into your strategic plan.

DEVELOPING A STRATEGIC PLAN

Develop a comprehensive strategic plan for earning money on Meta platforms. Outline the steps and actions you need to take to achieve your financial goals. Consider factors such as content creation schedules, marketing and promotion strategies, community engagement, and platform-specific optimizations. Your strategic plan should be adaptable to changes in the Meta landscape and reflect your ongoing learning and growth.

BUILDING A SUPPORT NETWORK

Building a support network is crucial for success on Meta platforms. Connect with like-minded creators, entrepreneurs, and industry professionals who can provide guidance, support, and collaboration opportunities. Engage in communities and forums dedicated to Meta platforms to learn from others and stay updated on the latest trends and strategies.

03 CREATING CAPTIVATING CONTENT SECTION

Chapter three focuses on the art of creating captivating content on Meta platforms. By mastering content creation techniques, understanding the importance of quality, originality, and relevance, and leveraging storytelling and visual elements, you can engage and captivate your audience. The chapter emphasizes the need to tailor your content to the specific Meta platform while also staying true to your authentic self. By consistently delivering high-quality, original, and visually appealing content, you will establish yourself as a captivating creator within the Meta metaverse.

Mastering content creation techniques for Meta platforms.

EMBRACE THE UNIQUE FEATURES OF META PLATFORMS

To create captivating content on Meta platforms, it is crucial to understand and leverage the unique features and capabilities of each platform. Whether it's Meta Social, Meta Horizon, or other emerging platforms, familiarize yourself with the tools, effects, and interactive elements available. Experiment with these features to enhance the engagement and immersive experience for your audience.

TAILOR YOUR CONTENT TO THE PLATFORM

Each Meta platform has its own style and user base. Tailor your content to align with the preferences and expectations of the platform's audience. Study successful creators within your niche and analyze the type of content they produce. Take inspiration from their approach while adding your unique touch to stand out from the crowd.

CONSISTENCY AND FREQUENCY

Consistency and frequency are key to maintaining an engaged audience on Meta platforms. Develop a content creation schedule and stick to it. Whether it's daily, weekly, or biweekly, ensure you consistently deliver content to keep your audience hooked. Regular updates also increase your visibility and relevance within the platform's algorithms. Section 2: Understanding the importance of quality, originality, and relevance

QUALITY OVER QUANTITY

While consistency is important, prioritize quality over quantity when creating content for Meta platforms. Ensure that your content is well-crafted, visually appealing, and offers value to your audience. Invest time and effort into refining your skills and techniques to produce high-quality content that stands out amidst the sea of content available on Meta platforms.

BE ORIGINAL AND AUTHENTIC

Originality and authenticity are crucial for capturing the attention of your audience. Avoid copying or imitating others' content. Instead, bring your unique perspective, ideas, and experiences to your creations. Showcasing your authentic self will help you build a loyal and engaged following on Meta platforms.

STAY RELEVANT AND EVOLVE

The Meta landscape is dynamic and constantly evolving. Stay updated with the latest trends, features, and user preferences within your niche. Adapt your content strategy to remain relevant and capitalize on emerging opportunities. Consistently seek feedback from your audience and iterate on your content to meet their evolving needs and expectations.

Leveraging storytelling and visual elements to engage your audience.

HARNESS THE POWER OF STORYTELLING

Storytelling is a powerful tool for creating captivating content on Meta platforms. Craft narratives that resonate with your audience and evoke emotions. Whether it's through written captions, immersive virtual experiences, or visual storytelling techniques, weave compelling stories that captivate and engage your audience.

ENGAGE WITH VISUAL ELEMENTS

Visual elements play a vital role in capturing and retaining the attention of your audience. Experiment with different visual techniques such as vibrant colors, creative compositions, and eye-catching designs. Utilize visual effects and filters available on Meta platforms to enhance the visual appeal of your content. Incorporate visually engaging elements such as animations, 3D models, or virtual reality experiences to create a memorable and immersive experience for your audience.

04 MONETIZATION STRATEGIES ON META SECTION

Chapter four steps into the various monetization strategies on Meta platforms. By exploring opportunities such as advertising, sponsorships, brand collaborations, and affiliate marketing, creators can leverage their presence to generate income. It emphasizes the importance of understanding the terms and conditions set by the platform, including revenue sharing models and payment methods. By strategically monetizing your presence on Meta platforms, you can turn your passion into a sustainable source of income while delivering valuable content to your audience.

Exploring the various ways to monetize your presence on Meta platforms.

UNDERSTANDING MONETIZATION OPPORTUNITIES

Meta platforms offer a range of opportunities for creators to monetize their presence. From advertising to sponsorships, brand collaborations, and affiliate marketing, it is essential to explore and understand the different avenues available. Each platform may have specific guidelines and requirements for monetization, so familiarize yourself with their policies and terms.

ADVERTISING ON META PLATFORMS

Advertising is a common and effective method to monetize your presence on Meta platforms. Platforms like Meta Social offer advertising options such as in-feed ads, sponsored posts, or targeted ads. Familiarize yourself with the advertising tools and guidelines provided by the platform and create engaging and relevant ad content that resonates with your audience.

Leveraging sponsorships, brand collaborations, and affiliate marketing.

SPONSORSHIPS AND BRAND COLLABORATIONS

Sponsorships and brand collaborations are another popular way to monetize your presence on Meta platforms. As your audience grows, you can attract brands and businesses interested in reaching your followers. Establish partnerships with relevant brands that align with your content and values. Negotiate sponsorship deals that include sponsored content, product placements, or brand endorsements. Remember to maintain transparency and authenticity in your collaborations to build trust with your audience.

AFFILIATE MARKETING

Affiliate marketing is a performance-based strategy where you earn a commission for promoting and driving sales for products or services. Join affiliate programs relevant to your niche and incorporate affiliate links or discount codes into your content. When your audience makes a purchase through your referral, you earn a commission. Ensure you disclose your affiliate partnerships to maintain transparency with your audience.

Understanding the terms and conditions, revenue sharing, and payment methods.

UNDERSTANDING TERMS AND CONDITIONS

Each Meta platform has its own terms and conditions for monetization. It is crucial to carefully read and understand these terms to ensure compliance. Pay attention to guidelines regarding content creation, advertising policies, sponsored content disclosures, and any restrictions on monetization activities. Failure to adhere to these guidelines may result in penalties or loss of monetization privileges.

REVENUE SHARING AND PAYMENT METHODS

Meta platforms typically have revenue sharing models where creators receive a percentage of the revenue generated through monetization activities. Familiarize yourself with the platform's revenue sharing policies, including the percentage you will receive and any minimum payout thresholds. Additionally, explore the available payment methods for receiving your earnings, such as direct bank transfers, PayPal, or other supported payment platforms.

05 GROWING YOUR META AUDIENCE

Chapter five focuses on effective strategies for growing your Meta audience. By leveraging social media, optimizing for search engines, and actively building a community, you can attract a larger audience. Additionally, it emphasizes the importance of consistency, authenticity, and interaction in order to keep your audience engaged and foster long-term relationships. By implementing these strategies, you can expand your reach, increase your followers, and create a thriving Meta audience.

Implementing effective strategies to increase your followers and engagement.

SETTING CLEAR GOALS

Before diving into audience growth strategies, it is important to set clear goals for your Meta presence. Determine what you want to achieve, whether it's increasing followers, improving engagement, or reaching a specific target audience. Having clear goals will guide your strategies and help you measure your progress.

LEVERAGING SOCIAL MEDIA

Social media platforms are powerful tools for expanding your Meta audience. Utilize platforms like Twitter, Instagram, and Facebook to promote your Meta content, engage with your audience, and attract new followers. Share teasers, highlights, and behind-the-scenes content to create curiosity and encourage your social media followers to check out your Meta presence.

Leveraging SEO and Community Building

OPTIMIZING FOR SEARCH ENGINES

Optimizing your Meta presence for search engines can help attract organic traffic and grow your audience. Research relevant keywords and incorporate them into your Meta profile, posts, and descriptions. Use descriptive titles and tags for your content and consider writing keyword-rich meta descriptions. Additionally, engage in keyword research to identify trending topics and create content that aligns with popular search queries.

ENGAGING IN COMMUNITY BUILDING

Building a community around your Meta presence is crucial for audience growth. Engage with your existing followers by responding to comments, asking for feedback, and creating a sense of belonging. Encourage discussions and collaboration among your audience members. Actively participate in Meta groups and communities related to your niche to expand your reach and connect with like-minded individuals.

Understanding the importance of consistency, authenticity, and interaction will help you build a loyal community of followers.

CONSISTENCY IN CONTENT CREATION

Consistency is key to growing your Meta audience. Regularly create and publish high-quality content that aligns with your niche and resonates with your target audience. Develop a content calendar or schedule to ensure a consistent flow of posts. Consistency builds trust and keeps your audience engaged and coming back for more.

AUTHENTICITY AND TRANSPARENCY

Authenticity is essential for building a loyal and engaged Meta audience. Be genuine and true to yourself in your content. Share personal stories, experiences, and insights that are unique to you. Transparency is equally important, especially when engaging in sponsored content or affiliate marketing. Be upfront about partnerships and clearly disclose any sponsored content or affiliate links to maintain trust with your audience.

ACTIVE INTERACTION AND ENGAGEMENT

Interacting with your audience is crucial for audience growth and retention. Respond to comments, messages, and inquiries promptly. Ask questions, encourage discussions, and show genuine interest in your audience's opinions and experiences. Engage in meaningful conversations and foster a sense of community. Active interaction and engagement will help you build relationships and attract new followers.

06 BUILDING A PERSONAL BRAND ON META

Chapter six focuses on building a personal brand on Meta. By crafting a unique brand identity, establishing yourself as an authority in your niche, and leveraging your personal brand to attract opportunities and partnerships, you can create a strong presence and position yourself for success on Meta. Building a personal brand takes time and effort, but with consistency and authenticity, you can create a brand that stands out and attracts a loyal following.

Crafting a unique and recognizable brand identity.

UNDERSTANDING YOUR BRAND IDENTITY

Building a strong personal brand on Meta starts with understanding who you are and what you want to be known for. Define your values, passions, and unique qualities that set you apart from others. Identify your target audience and tailor your content and messaging to resonate with them.

CREATING A CONSISTENT VISUAL IDENTITY

Visual elements play a crucial role in creating a recognizable brand identity on Meta. Design a logo, choose a color palette, and select fonts that align with your brand personality. Use these visual elements consistently across your Meta profile, posts, and promotional materials to establish a cohesive and professional look.

ESTABLISHING YOURSELF AS AN AUTHORITY IN YOUR NICHE

Sharing Valuable and Expert Content: To establish yourself as an authority in your niche, consistently create and share valuable content that showcases your expertise. Provide informative and actionable insights, tips, and advice that your audience can benefit from. Demonstrate your knowledge and passion for your niche through well-researched and well-presented content.

COLLABORATING WITH INFLUENCERS AND EXPERTS:

Collaborating with influencers and experts in your niche can help boost your credibility and expand your reach. Seek opportunities to collaborate on joint projects, guest post on established blogs or podcasts, or participate in industry events and conferences. These collaborations can introduce you to new audiences and position you as a trusted authority in your field.

Leveraging your personal brand to attract opportunities and partnerships.

NETWORKING AND BUILDING RELATIONSHIPS

Networking is essential for building your personal brand and attracting opportunities. Engage with other creators, industry professionals, and potential collaborators on Meta and other social media platforms. Attend virtual events, join relevant groups and communities, and actively participate in conversations. Building genuine relationships can lead to valuable partnerships, collaborations, and opportunities.

SHOWCASING YOUR ACHIEVEMENTS AND EXPERTISE

Highlight your achievements, accolades, and experiences on your Meta profile and in your content. Share success stories, case studies, and testimonials from satisfied clients or customers. Demonstrating your expertise and the impact you have made in your niche will attract attention and establish you as a go-to authority.

LEVERAGING SPONSORSHIPS AND PARTNERSHIPS

As your personal brand grows, you may attract opportunities for sponsorships and partnerships. Carefully choose partnerships that align with your brand values and resonate with your audience. Collaborate with brands and organizations that can provide value to your audience while also benefiting your personal brand. These partnerships can not only generate income but also enhance your brand's visibility and credibility.

07 EXPANDING YOUR REACH ON META

Chapter seven explores strategies for expanding your reach on Meta. By leveraging cross-platform promotion and collaboration, understanding Meta's algorithm and features, and exploring the use of hashtags, trends, and viral content, you can reach a wider audience and increase your visibility on the platform. Remember to stay authentic, consistent, and engage with your audience to build a loyal following and continue growing your personal brand on Meta.

Strategies for cross-platform promotion and collaboration.

LEVERAGING MULTIPLE SOCIAL MEDIA PLATFORMS

Expanding your reach on Meta involves utilizing other social media platforms to promote your content and attract a wider audience. Cross-promote your Meta profile and content on platforms like Instagram, Twitter, YouTube, and LinkedIn. Share teasers, snippets, or behind-the-scenes content to generate curiosity and encourage your existing followers on other platforms to engage with you on Meta.

COLLABORATING WITH OTHER CREATORS

Collaborating with other creators can help expand your reach and introduce your content to new audiences. Seek out creators in your niche or complementary niches and explore collaboration opportunities. Collaborative content, such as joint live streams, interviews, or guest appearances, can expose you to a larger audience and create mutually beneficial relationships with other creators.

Leveraging Meta's algorithm and features to increase visibility.

UNDERSTANDING META'S ALGORITHM

To expand your reach on Meta, it's important to understand how the platform's algorithm works. Pay attention to factors such as engagement, comments, and shares, as they influence the visibility of your content. Create engaging and valuable content that encourages interaction and prompts meaningful conversations to increase your chances of appearing in users' feeds.

UTILIZING META'S FEATURES

Meta offers various features that can help increase your visibility. Explore features like Meta Live, Meta Rooms, and Meta Groups to engage with your audience in real-time and foster a sense of community. Take advantage of Meta's video and audio capabilities to create compelling content that stands out in users' feeds.

Exploring the use of hashtags, trends, and viral content to reach a wider audience.

HARNESSING THE POWER OF HASHTAGS

Hashtags play a crucial role in increasing the discoverability of your content on Meta. Research popular hashtags in your niche and incorporate them strategically into your posts. Additionally, create branded hashtags specific to your personal brand to encourage user-generated content and increase engagement.

RIDING THE WAVE OF TRENDS

Stay informed about the latest trends and topics on Meta and align your content with them. By participating in trending conversations and using relevant hashtags, you can increase your chances of reaching a wider audience and gaining exposure.

CREATING VIRAL-WORTHY CONTENT

Creating content with the potential to go viral can significantly expand your reach on Meta. Pay attention to viral content trends, such as challenges, memes, or creative formats, and put your unique spin on them. Engage with your audience by creating shareable and relatable content that resonates with them on an emotional level.

08 NAVIGATING LEGAL AND FINANCIAL

Chapter eight provides insights into navigating legal and financial considerations as a content creator on Meta. By understanding the legal and tax implications, protecting intellectual property, and developing sound financial habits, you can ensure compliance, safeguard your creative works, and pave the way for long-term success on the platform. Remember to seek professional advice, stay informed about platform policies, and make informed financial decisions to maximize your earning potential on Meta.

Understanding the legal and tax implications of earning money on Meta.

CONSULTATION WITH LEGAL AND TAX PROFESSIONALS

Earning money on Meta may have legal and tax implications. It is essential to consult with legal and tax professionals to understand the specific regulations and requirements in your jurisdiction. They can provide guidance on issues such as income reporting, tax obligations, and any necessary permits or licenses.

FAMILIARIZING YOURSELF WITH PLATFORM POLICIES

Meta has its own terms of service and community guidelines that you must adhere to when earning money on the platform. Familiarize yourself with these policies to ensure compliance and avoid potential legal issues. Stay updated on any changes or updates to the platform's policies to adjust your strategies accordingly.

Protecting intellectual property and managing copyright issues.

UNDERSTANDING INTELLECTUAL PROPERTY RIGHTS

As a content creator on Meta, it is crucial to understand intellectual property rights and how they apply to your content. Familiarize yourself with copyright laws and the protection they afford to original creative works. Ensure that you have the necessary rights or permissions for any third-party content you use in your creations.

MANAGING COPYRIGHT ISSUES

Monitor your content on Meta to identify any unauthorized use or infringement. If you encounter copyright violations, you can report them to Meta and take appropriate action to protect your intellectual property.

Consider registering your original works with relevant copyright authorities for additional protection.

Developing sound financial habits and practices for long-term success.

ESTABLISHING FINANCIAL GOALS

Define your financial goals and create a plan to achieve them. Set realistic targets for earning money on Meta and outline the steps required to reach those goals. Consider factors such as monetization options, audience engagement, and content diversification to maximize your revenue potential.

TRACKING AND MANAGING INCOME AND EXPENSES

Maintain accurate records of your income and expenses related to your activities on Meta. This will help you track your earnings, assess your profitability, and ensure compliance with tax obligations. Consider using accounting software or working with a financial professional to streamline your financial management processes.

DIVERSIFYING REVENUE STREAMS

Relying solely on one revenue stream may pose risks to your long-term financial success on Meta. Explore opportunities to diversify your income, such as sponsorships, brand partnerships, merchandise sales, and collaborations. Diversification can provide stability and mitigate the impact of fluctuations in any single income source.

09 LEGAL AND FINANCIAL CONSIDERATIONS

Chapter nine provides valuable insights into the legal and financial considerations of earning money on Meta. By understanding your legal responsibilities, navigating copyright and intellectual property issues, and managing taxes and financial planning, you can ensure compliance, protect your creative works, and pave the way for long-term success on the platform. Remember to seek professional advice, stay informed about legal and licensing requirements, and implement effective financial strategies to maximize your earning potential on Meta.

Understanding the legal obligations and responsibilities of earning money on Meta.

COMPLIANCE WITH PLATFORM POLICIES AND TERMS OF SERVICE

When earning money on Meta, it is important to familiarize yourself with the platform's policies and terms of service. Adhere to these guidelines to ensure compliance and avoid potential legal issues. Stay updated on any changes or updates to the platform's policies to adjust your strategies accordingly.

LEGAL OBLIGATIONS AND PERMITS

Depending on your location and the nature of your earnings on Meta, there may be legal obligations and permits you need to fulfill. Consult with legal professionals to understand the specific regulations and requirements in your jurisdiction. This may include obtaining business licenses and permits or registering as a self-employed individual.

Navigating copyright, intellectual property, and licensing issues.

COPYRIGHT AND INTELLECTUAL PROPERTY PROTECTION

As a content creator on Meta, it is crucial to understand copyright and intellectual property laws and how they apply to your work. Ensure that you have the necessary rights or permissions for any third-party content you use in your creations. Consider registering your original works with relevant copyright authorities for additional protection.

LICENSING AND PERMISSIONS

If you plan to use copyrighted or licensed material in your content, it is essential to obtain the necessary permissions or licenses. This includes music, images, videos, and any other copyrighted material. Research and understand the various licensing options available, such as Creative Commons, to ensure you are using content legally and ethically.

Managing taxes, reporting income, and financial planning for long-term success

TAX OBLIGATIONS AND REPORTING INCOME

Earning money on Meta may have tax implications. Consult with tax professionals to understand your tax obligations and reporting requirements. Keep accurate records of your income and expenses related to your activities on Meta to facilitate tax filing. Consider setting aside a portion of your earnings for taxes to avoid financial strain when tax season arrives.

FINANCIAL PLANNING FOR LONG-TERM SUCCESS

Develop sound financial habits and practices to ensure long-term success on Meta. Establish financial goals and create a comprehensive plan to achieve them. This includes budgeting, saving, and investing wisely. Consider working with financial advisors or professionals who specialize in digital content creators to optimize your financial planning strategies.

10 ADAPTING TO CHANGES AND STAYING AHEAD

Chapter ten emphasizes the importance of adapting to changes and staying ahead on Meta. By effectively dealing with algorithm changes and platform updates, embracing new trends and technologies, and cultivating resilience, adaptability, and continuous learning, content creators can maintain their competitive edge. Remember to stay informed, experiment with new features, and nurture a mindset of growth and improvement to thrive in the dynamic world of Meta.

Dealing with algorithm changes and platform updates on Meta.

UNDERSTANDING ALGORITHM CHANGES

The algorithms that govern content visibility and reach on Meta are constantly evolving. It is crucial to stay informed about algorithm changes and updates to adapt your content strategy accordingly. Keep an eye on official announcements, community forums, and industry news to understand how these changes may impact your content's performance.

ANALYZING AND ADJUSTING STRATEGIES

When algorithm changes occur, closely monitor the performance of your content. Analyze the metrics and engagement data to identify any patterns or trends. Adjust your content creation and distribution strategies based on the insights gathered. Experiment with different formats, keywords, and posting schedules to optimize your content's visibility and reach.

Embracing new trends, features, and technologies.

EMBRACING NEW TRENDS

To stay ahead on Meta, it is essential to keep up with the latest trends and user preferences. Stay connected with the Meta community, follow industry influencers, and engage with your audience to identify emerging trends. Incorporate these trends into your content strategy to maintain relevance and capture the attention of your target audience.

UTILIZING NEW FEATURES AND TECHNOLOGIES

Meta regularly introduces new features and technologies to enhance the user experience. Embrace these innovations and explore how they can benefit your content creation and engagement. Experiment with new features such as live streaming, augmented reality, or interactive elements to provide unique and engaging experiences for your audience.

Cultivating resilience, adaptability, and continuous learning.

CULTIVATING RESILIENCE

The digital landscape is dynamic and ever-changing. Cultivate resilience by adopting a growth mindset and embracing challenges as opportunities for learning and improvement. Stay positive and motivated, even in the face of setbacks or algorithmic fluctuations. Learn from failures and adapt your strategies accordingly.

EMBRACING ADAPTABILITY

Adaptability is key to staying ahead on Meta. Be open to change and willing to adjust your approach as needed. Continuously evaluate and refine your content strategy to align with the evolving needs and preferences of your audience. Embrace experimentation and be willing to step out of your comfort zone to discover new opportunities for growth.

COMMITTING TO CONTINUOUS LEARNING

The digital landscape is constantly evolving, and staying ahead requires a commitment to continuous learning. Stay curious and actively seek out new knowledge and skills related to content creation, marketing, and platform trends. Engage in industry webinars, workshops, and online courses to expand your expertise and stay ahead of the curve.

11 CASE STUDIES AND SUCCESS STORIES

Chapter eleven goes into real-life case studies and success stories of individuals who have achieved financial success on Meta platforms. By learning from their strategies, mistakes, and triumphs, content creators can gain valuable insights and inspiration to enhance their own journeys. Through these stories, we highlight effective monetization strategies, analyze lessons learned, and provide actionable advice for content creators aiming to achieve financial success on Meta.

Inspiring Stories of Financial Success on Meta Platforms

INTRODUCTION TO SUCCESS STORIES

In this chapter, we delve into inspiring case studies of individuals who have achieved significant financial success on Meta platforms. These success stories showcase how ordinary people have leveraged the power of Meta to achieve their financial goals and create a sustainable income stream.

THE JOURNEY OF CONTENT CREATOR X

In this case study, we explore the journey of Content Creator X, who started from scratch and built a thriving online business on a Meta platform. We dive into their initial struggles, the strategies they employed, and the turning points that led to their financial success. Through their story, we gain insights into the steps they took to monetize their content effectively.

THE RISE OF ENTREPRENEUR Y

Entrepreneur Y is another success story that we examine in this section. We uncover how they identified a gap in the market and utilized Meta platforms to launch a successful business. We analyze their marketing tactics, customer engagement strategies, and the role Meta played in scaling their business to new heights.

Learning from Strategies, Mistakes, and Triumphs

STRATEGIES FOR MONETIZING CONTENT

Through the case studies, we highlight the strategies employed by successful individuals to monetize their content effectively. We explore various revenue streams, such as advertising, sponsored content, product sales, and subscription models. By understanding their approaches, content creators can gain valuable insights and apply them to their own monetization strategies.

MISTAKES AND LESSONS LEARNED

No success story is without its share of challenges and mistakes. We analyze the hurdles faced by the individuals in our case studies and the lessons they learned along the way. By understanding their missteps, content creators can avoid common pitfalls and make informed decisions to navigate their own journeys to financial success on Meta platforms.

Drawing Valuable Insights and Inspiration

EXTRACTING KEY INSIGHTS

Throughout this chapter, we extract key insights from the success stories and distill them into actionable advice. We identify common themes, strategies, and mindsets that contributed to the financial success of these individuals. By drawing on these insights, content creators can enhance their own approaches and increase their chances of achieving success on Meta platforms.

FINDING INSPIRATION

Lastly, we emphasize the importance of finding inspiration in real-life examples. The success stories presented in this chapter serve as a source of motivation and encouragement for content creators. They demonstrate that with determination, strategic thinking, and the right approach, financial success on Meta platforms is within reach for anyone willing to put in the effort.

12 THE FUTURE OF EARNING MONEY ON META

Chapter twelve examines the future of earning money on Meta platforms. By exploring future trends and opportunities, predicting the evolution of Meta platforms, and understanding their impact on the digital economy, individuals can seize new opportunities and stay ahead of the curve. This chapter emphasizes the importance of identifying new revenue streams, embracing emerging technologies, and navigating regulatory and ethical considerations. By staying informed and adaptable, individuals can position themselves for success in the ever-evolving Meta landscape.

Exploring Future Trends and Opportunities

INTRODUCTION TO THE FUTURE OF EARNING MONEY ON META

In this chapter, we explore the exciting possibilities and emerging trends in the Meta landscape. We delve into the future of earning money on Meta platforms and how individuals can position themselves to seize new opportunities in this evolving digital economy.

PREDICTING THE EVOLUTION OF META PLATFORMS

We analyze the current state of Meta platforms and predict how they will evolve in the future. We examine the advancements in technology, user behavior, and market dynamics that will shape the Meta landscape. By understanding these trends, individuals can anticipate the changes that lie ahead and adapt their strategies accordingly.

The Impact on the Digital Economy

THE INFLUENCE OF META ON THE DIGITAL ECONOMY

Meta platforms have already disrupted traditional industries and transformed the way we interact, consume content, and do business. In this section, we delve into the broader impact of Meta on the digital economy. We analyze the effects on industries such as entertainment, marketing, e-commerce, education, and more. By understanding these impacts, individuals can align their strategies with the changing landscape and capitalize on new opportunities.

THE RISE OF THE CREATOR ECONOMY

One of the significant trends brought forth by Meta platforms is the rise of the creator economy. We explore how individuals can leverage their skills, expertise, and creativity to monetize their content and build sustainable income streams. We discuss the growing importance of personal branding, community engagement, and content monetization strategies in the creator economy.

Seizing New Opportunities and Staying Ahead

IDENTIFYING NEW REVENUE STREAMS

As Meta platforms continue to evolve, new revenue streams will emerge. We explore potential avenues for earning money on Meta, such as virtual reality experiences, augmented reality advertising, NFTs, and more. By identifying these new revenue streams, individuals can stay ahead of the curve and adapt their monetization strategies to capitalize on emerging opportunities.

EMBRACING EMERGING TECHNOLOGIES

We discuss the role of emerging technologies, such as artificial intelligence, blockchain, and virtual reality, in shaping the future of earning money on Meta platforms. We explore how these technologies can enhance user experiences, enable new forms of content creation and monetization, and create innovative business models. By embracing these technologies, individuals can position themselves at the forefront of the evolving Meta landscape.

NAVIGATING REGULATORY AND ETHICAL CONSIDERATIONS

As Meta platforms gain more prominence, regulatory and ethical considerations come into play. We discuss the evolving regulatory landscape and the importance of ethical practices in the Meta ecosystem. We provide insights on how individuals can navigate these considerations while building their businesses and maintaining trust with their audience.

TURNING PASSION INTO A THRIVING COMMUNITY: OUR JOURNEY TO SUCCESS ON META

By prioritizing our audience's needs and desires, we built a loyal following that eagerly awaited each new piece of content we produced. Our dedication and strategic approach paid off. The Facebook group page became a go-to destination for those seeking meaningful discussions and connections, while the YouTube channel became a trusted source of valuable content. Through our passion, authenticity, and commitment to delivering quality, we transformed our hobbies into a thriving online presence. It wasn't just about the numbers for us. We genuinely enjoyed the interactions and connections we made through our Facebook group and YouTube channel. We celebrated the success of our community members and supported their growth as well.

Together, we formed a supportive network of creators and enthusiasts, inspiring each other to reach new heights. As our journey continued, we expanded our content offerings and explored new platforms to reach even more people. We never lost sight of our initial goal of sharing our unique perspective with the world. With each new challenge, we embraced the opportunity to learn, adapt, and grow as content creators, and so the story and the growth of our Facebook group page and YouTube channel stand as a testament to the power of passion, dedication, and community. It shows that by creating valuable and authentic content, building a supportive community, and continually striving for growth, anyone can turn their passion into a platform that reaches and inspires others.

This book gives you knowledge on growing successful teams and groups related to meta, and we are living proof that you can make money on meta with your team. We had a deep passion for creating content and wanted to share unique perspectives with the world. With that in mind, we set out on a journey to grow our Facebook group page and YouTube channel using our captivating content. Andi Scott and I started out by carefully curating our content to reflect our interests and expertise. We brainstormed ideas, researched trends, and poured our heart and soul into every piece we created. Whether it was engaging blog posts, informative videos, or thought-provoking discussions, we aimed to provide value and entertainment to our audience and grow our Facebook group page. We invited friends, family, and acquaintances who shared similar interests to join the group. To attract new members, we actively participated in relevant online communities, sharing valuable insights and promoting our group as a hub for like-minded individuals. As the group began to grow, we established a sense of community by encouraging discussions and organizing interactive events. We created polls, asked thought-provoking questions, and facilitated conversations that resonated with our audience, also offering stars for food challenges, best pictures, and more.

Through our dedication and authenticity, we cultivated an engaged and supportive community within our Facebook group. Simultaneously, the Get Money Meta group focused on expanding our presence on YouTube. We uploaded high-quality videos regularly, ensuring each one was visually appealing and provided valuable information or entertainment. To attract viewers, we optimized our video titles, descriptions, and tags with relevant keywords, making it easier for people to discover the content. To further amplify our reach, we collaborated with other content creators in our niche. We participated in guest interviews, collaborated on joint projects, and cross-promoted each other's channels. These collaborations not only introduced us to new audiences but also brought fresh perspectives and ideas to our content.

Get Money Meta

As our Facebook group and YouTube channel gained momentum, we started monetizing our efforts. We joined YouTube's Partner Program, allowing us to earn revenue through advertisements displayed on the videos. We explored sponsorship opportunities, partnering with brands that aligned with our values and resonated with our audience. With our growing success, we realized the importance of nurturing our community. We actively listened to our audience's feedback, responding to comments and messages and incorporating their suggestions into our content.

BUILDING A HIGH-PERFORMING TEAM

Building a high-performing team is essential for achieving success in any endeavor. A team that works together and effectively can accomplish remarkable goals and drive an organization forward. To build and nurture such a team, there are several key pieces of advice to consider.

First, define your vision and goals. Clearly articulate them to provide a sense of purpose and direction for your team. This clarity will help align everyone's efforts towards a common purpose, ensuring that all team members are working towards the same goal.

Next, hire the right people. Take the time to carefully select team members who not only possess the necessary skills and qualifications but also align with your vision, values, and culture. Look for individuals who demonstrate a growth mindset, adaptability, and a strong work ethic. The right mix of skills and attitudes can make a significant difference in team dynamics and performance.

Promote collaboration and communication by establishing clear roles and responsibilities to minimize confusion and promote accountability. Create an environment where open and honest communication is encouraged, and create a culture of active listening, feedback, and constructive dialogue. When team members feel heard and valued, they are more likely to contribute effectively and work together in a sense where they will flow together.

Encourage continuous learning and development. Invest in the growth and development of your team members by providing training programs, workshops, and resources. Help them acquire new skills and knowledge so they can excel in their roles. A commitment to continuous learning keeps the team dynamic and adaptable to changes and challenges.

Promote a positive and supportive work environment where team members feel valued, respected, and empowered. Encourage teamwork, collaboration, and a sense of belonging. A positive environment boosts morale and fosters a culture where everyone is motivated to give their best.

Set clear expectations and goals by clearly communicating what is expected of each team member and setting SMART goals that are specific, measurable, achievable, relevant, and time-bound. This approach provides clarity and motivation, helping team members understand their roles in achieving the team's objectives.

Provide regular feedback and recognition. Give timely and constructive feedback to help your team members grow and improve. Recognize and reward their achievements and contributions to boost morale and motivation. Positive reinforcement can drive continuous improvement and high performance. Creating a supportive and inclusive team environment can help develop collaboration and innovation. Encouraging open communication and celebrating diversity can lead to increased creativity and productivity within the team.

Support innovation and creativity by encouraging your team members to think outside the box and explore new ideas. Create a culture that values innovation, experimentation, and continuous improvement. Innovation can lead to breakthroughs that drive the team and the organization forward. By establishing a culture of innovation, you can empower your team to come up with creative solutions to challenges and stay ahead of the competition. Encourage open communication and collaboration to spark new ideas and drive success.

Lead by example. Be a role model for your team by demonstrating the values, behaviors, and work ethic you expect from them. Show empathy, integrity, and transparency in your actions and decisions. A leader who walks the talk inspires the team to follow suit. By setting high standards for yourself, you set the bar for your team and motivate them to strive for excellence. Remember to provide support and recognition for their efforts, building a positive and productive work environment. Ultimately, a strong leader cultivates a culture of continuous improvement and innovation that propels the organization towards success.

The final thing to do is to establish a healthy work-life balance. Encourage a healthy work-life balance by promoting flexible work arrangements, providing support for personal well-being, and recognizing the importance of rest and rejuvenation. A balanced team is a more productive and happier team. By prioritizing work-life balance, those who are on your team will feel valued and supported, leading to increased work satisfaction and overall well-being. This will result in higher levels of productivity and creativity within the team, ultimately benefiting the organization as a whole.

Remember, building a high-performance team is an ongoing process. Continuously invest in your team's growth and development, adapt to changing circumstances, and create a culture of continuous learning and improvement. By doing so, you create a resilient and high-performing team capable of achieving extraordinary results.

ABOUT THE AUTHOR

Errol Hassell, also known as Wave Moneyy, is the CEO and Founder of Get Money Meta, a Facebook group of 20K members. Their common goal within this community is to learn how to make money from social media and networking together. His debut book, Get Money Meta: Mastering the Meta Marketplace, provides valuable insights and strategies for individuals looking to maximize their earning potential in the digital age. Through his leadership and expertise, Errol Hassell has helped countless individuals achieve financial success through social media platforms.

Made in the USA
Monee, IL
13 September 2026

62980097R00036